4◉ DAYS THROUGH

ACTS

THE REVOLUTION OF FAITH

STUDY GUIDE + STREAMING VIDEO | 6 SESSIONS

RANDY FRAZEE

WITH KEVIN AND SHERRY HARNEY

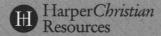

Harper*Christian*
Resources

40 Days Through the Book: Acts Study Guide
© 2023 by Randy Frazee

Published in Grand Rapids, Michigan, by HarperChristian Resources. HarperChristian Resources is a registered trademark of HarperCollins Christian Publishing, Inc.

Requests for information should be addressed to customercare@harpercollins.com.

ISBN 978-0-310-15976-6 (softcover)
ISBN 978-0-310-15977-3 (ebook)

HarperChristian Resources titles may be purchased in bulk for church, business, fundraising, or ministry use. For information, please e-mail ResourceSpecialist@ ChurchSource.com.

Published in association with Don Gates of the literary agency The Gates Group— www.the-gatesgroup.com.

First Printing March 2023 / Printed in the United States of America

24 25 26 27 28 LBC 6 5 4 3 2

CONTENTS

HOW TO USE THIS GUIDE

SCOPE AND SEQUENCE

Welcome to the *40 Days Through the Book* study on the book of Acts! During the course of the next six weeks, you and your fellow group members will embark on an in-depth exploration of the disciple Luke's message to believers in the Church. During this study, you will learn when he wrote the book, approximately when it was written, and the background and context in which it was written. But, more importantly, through the teaching by Randy Frazee, you will explore the key themes that Luke relates in the book—and how his teachings apply to you today.

SESSION OUTLINE

The *40 Days Through the Book* video and study guide are designed to be experienced both in group settings (such as a Bible study, Sunday school class, or small group gatherings) as well as in your individual study time. Each session begins with an introductory reading and question. You will then watch the video message. (Play the DVD or refer to the instructions on the inside front cover on how to access the sessions at any time through streaming.) An outline has been provided in the guide for you to take notes and gather your reflections as you watch the video. Next, if you are doing this study with a group, you will engage in a time of directed discussion, review the memory verses for the week, and close with a time of prayer. (Note that if your group is larger, you may wish to watch the videos together and then break into smaller groups of four to six people, to ensure that everyone has time to participate in discussions.)

40-DAY JOURNEY

What is truly unique about this study, and all of the other studies in the *40 Days Through the Book* series, are the daily learning resources that will lead you into a deeper engagement with the text. Each week, you will be given a set of daily readings, with accompanying reflection questions, to help you explore the material that you covered during your group time.

The first day's reading will focus on the key verse to memorize for the week. In the other weekly readings, you will be invited to read a passage from the book of Acts, reflect on the text, and then respond with some guided journal questions. On the final day, you will review the key verse again and recite it from memory. As you work through the six weeks' worth of material in this section, you will read (and, in some cases, reread) the entire book of Acts.

Now, you may be wondering why you will be doing this over the course of *forty* days. Certainly, there is nothing special about that number. But there is something biblical about it. In the Bible, the number forty typically designates a time of *testing*. Noah was in the ark for forty days. Moses lived forty years in Egypt and another forty years in the desert before he led God's people. He spent forty days on Mount Sinai receiving God's laws and sent spies, for forty days, to investigate the land of Canaan. Later, God sent the prophet Jonah to warn ancient Nineveh, for forty days, that its destruction would come because of the people's sins.

Even more critically, in the New Testament we read that Jesus spent forty days in the wilderness, fasting and praying. It marked a critical transition point in his ministry—the place where he set about to fulfill the mission that God had intended. During this time Jesus was tested relentlessly by the enemy . . . and prevailed. When he returned to Galilee, he was a different person than the man who had entered into the wilderness forty days before. The same will be true for you as you commit to this forty-day journey through Acts.

GROUP FACILITATION

If you are doing this study with a group, everyone should have a copy of this study guide. Not only will this help you engage when your group is meeting, but it will also allow you to fully enter into the *40 Days* learning experience. Keep in mind the video, questions, and activities are simply tools to help you engage with the session. The real power and life-transformation will come as you dig into the Scriptures and seek to live out the truths you learn along the way.

Finally, you will need to appoint a leader or facilitator for the group who is responsible for starting the video teaching and for keeping track of time during discussions and activities. Leaders may also read questions aloud and monitor discussions, prompting participants to respond and ensuring that everyone has the opportunity to participate. For more thorough instructions on this role, see the Leader's Guide included at the back of this guide.

THE REVOLUTION OF FAITH

AUTHOR, DATE, AND LOCATION

Although neither the Gospel of Luke nor the Book of Acts has Luke's name directly attributed to it, there was unanimous consensus in the early Church that Luke the physician was the author of *both*. The Book of Luke is Part One and contains the story of Jesus' birth, life, ministry, death, resurrection and ascension back to heaven. The Book of Acts is Part Two of Luke's work and picks up right where the gospel finishes off. It tells the story of the ascension of Jesus and continues on with the birth, growth, and dramatic spread of the church from Jerusalem to the ends of the earth.

Both Luke and Acts were written to Luke's dear friend Theophilus (Luke 1:3 and Acts 1:1). Luke was most likely a Gentile (non-Jew) and he experienced parts of what we read in the Book of Acts firsthand. We know this because Luke writes in the first-person plural using "we" for almost a hundred verses of the Book of Acts. He was there! This means that Acts was written in the lifetime of Luke and he was there when many of these things happened.

THE BIG PICTURE

Before Jesus ascended to heaven (after his resurrection and appearances) he gave a very specific command to his followers. We find it at the very beginning of the Book of Acts:

> *"But you will receive power when the Holy Spirit comes on you; and you will be my witnesses in Jerusalem, and in all Judea and Samaria, and to the ends of the earth" (Acts 1:8).*

This was a call to a revolution of faith that would begin right where they lived, shopped, played, and worshipped (Jerusalem). It would spread to the surrounding community (Judea). The good news would also go to the places that many of the early followers of Jesus avoided and had no interest in visiting (Samaria). Finally, like a rapidly spreading contagion, the message, truth, and power of Jesus would extend to the ends of the earth!

As you read the book of Acts, you will discover that the structure of the narrative actually follows the order found in Acts 1:8. Along the way Luke gives continual updates on how this mission was being carried out and the success of God's people as they followed the leading of the Holy Spirit. The Book of Acts is a joyful celebration of how God's revolutionary message was unstoppable and contagious.

This inspiring book of the Bible is encouraging and filled with hope. Because the God we meet in the Scriptures is the same yesterday, today, and forever, we can live with true optimism. We follow the same Messiah that led the early church. We are filled with the same Spirit of power who used his church to transform the ancient world. We worship the same God who loves with so much passion that he sent his one and only Son to give his life for our salvation (John 3:16).

When we come to the end of chapter 28 of Acts, we realize that the completion of this account of the birth and growth of the church is *not* the end of the story. It is a new beginning. We are writing Acts chapter 29 right now. The church is still alive and powerful! God is on the move. If we are willing to follow the leading of the Holy Spirit, we can see the same revolution of faith continue in our world today.

EPIC THEMES

There are several themes in Acts that are worthy of our focus. Some of these include:

The Church is more dynamic than we dream. The church that Jesus started is not buildings scattered around a community. It is not a collection of rules and regulations or a religious structure. The church is the revolutionary people of God bringing the good news of Jesus from where they are to the ends of the earth (Acts 1:1–6:7).

The journey of following Jesus and spreading his love will demand sacrifice and suffering. From the very beginning of the Church, God's people discovered that there would be battles and struggles. In many situations, the suffering of God's people led to the spread of the world-changing message of God's grace (Acts 6:8–9:31).

How Christians live and love has direct impact on the success of the revolution Jesus started. Christians are not flawless but we are called to love, serve, care and reflect the heart and very presence of Jesus. As the people of God live as the saints of God, the truth of Jesus spreads quickly in a hurting and broken world (Acts 9:32–12:24).

Grace is the secret sauce of God's revolution. We live in a graceless and conflicted world. It has always been this way. When God's people hold to the truth and wrap it in the amazing grace of Jesus the Messiah, people of all sorts are willing to investigate the person of Jesus and the mission of the church. When this happens, the revolution of faith continues (Acts 12:25–16:5).

The church is God's vehicle to spread the good news of Jesus next door and to the ends of the earth. There is a contagious nature to the love of God and grace that Jesus came to unleash. Christians are called to get near people from every walk of life . . . close enough to spread the viral goodness of our God (Acts 16:6–19:20).

God's way and not my way! It is easy to slip into a mentality that says, "I will do God's will my way." If we are going to be part of the call to share the revolutionary faith that Jesus brought into the world, we must learn to do it his way. Humble surrender is essential if this is going to happen. As we count the cost, follow Jesus' ways, and sacrifice for our Savior, his good news will spread next door and to the ends of the earth (Acts 19:21–28:31).

There is reason for confident optimism about the future of the church. God's plan to reach the whole world with his love, truth, and hope is still intact. There might be cultural resistance and bumps along the way but as you read through the Book of Acts you will quickly realize that this has always been the case. Surprisingly, you will discover that there was greater resistance to the message of Jesus 2,000 years ago than there is in most places today. As you dig into this study, you will hear a consistent invitation to join the revolution of faith that Jesus started two millennia ago. If you are willing to press passionately into this study, you will find yourself encouraged, hopeful and engaged in the work of Jesus in new and exciting ways.

HERE'S THE CHURCH

ACTS 1:1–6:7

Many people see churches as a series of disconnected and random buildings scattered around their town, city, or village. God sees the church as his united and revolutionary people placed in every part of our world. The church is not an antiquated religious organization. It is a living and dynamic body of God's people who continue to grow and transform the world for the glory of Jesus.

WELCOME

Things that are common and right in front of us are often greatly misunderstood. Think about the sun. We see it all the time so we assume we know all about it. But, did you know the sun is 864,000 miles in diameter and is 109 times *wider* than our earth? How many planets the size of the earth do you think could fit inside the sun? The answer will blow your mind! It is 1,300,000! In other words, the sun is HUGE! How hot is the sun? Look at it this way, water boils at 212 degrees Fahrenheit. That's hot! But at the core, the sun is about 27,000,000 degrees Fahrenheit. It is hard for us to even imagine that kind of ferocious heat. Maybe we don't know as much about the sun as we thought we did.

The church is a lot like that. There are churches all over the place. Many people who are doing this 40 Day Study through Acts have been part of the church their whole life. Because it is so familiar to many people, there is a sense that we understand the church. But there is a whole lot more to the church than most of us begin to dream.

Many people see the church as primarily a human-led organization. Churches hold worship services, ask for offerings, do weddings, and bury people. Though this might be true, there is so much more. Churches are Holy Spirit infused living organisms that are dynamic, alive, and changing the world around them.

Countless people think of the church as dying or dead. The truth is, the global church is growing, expanding, and still fulfilling the mission Jesus declared two thousand years ago. There are more followers of Jesus in the world today than in any time in history and there is a larger percentage of Americans who attend church now than there were at the turn of the twentieth century.

Some people see the church as a remnant of the past that

will soon evaporate and disappear into the rear-view mirror of history. God sees his church as a revolutionary movement that will continue to bring global transformation until Jesus comes again in glory.

Yes, the church has been around for a long time. Indeed, there are lots of church buildings around your community. No doubt, there are challenges facing the church in our modern world. But don't let anyone fool you. The church is still God's plan to bring the love, grace, and truth of heaven to our broken world.

The sun is bigger and hotter than most of us recognize. So is the church! Infused by the very power of heaven, the church is alive and active in our world and more powerful than any of us could imagine.

SHARE

What was your perception of the church when you were a child, and how has it changed through the years?

WATCH

Play the video for session one. (Play the DVD or see the instructions on the inside front cover on how to access the sessions through streaming.) As you watch, use the following outline to record any thoughts, questions, or key points that stand out to you.

A Sunday School lesson you will never forget. Here's the church . . .

Defining the word "Revolution"

Revolution = A complete change (Acts 1:1–8)

Meeting Dr. Luke, the author of the Book of Acts

The person and power of the Holy Spirit

The mission of the church (expanding to the ends of the earth)

Insights from Dr. Rodney Stark

Revolution = A complete circle

A powerful movement of the Holy Spirit

A radical change in the life of Peter

Small gatherings with massive impact

The life of the church

Fellowship and breaking bread

Apostolic teaching and prayer

Radical giving and serving

Numerical growth (More followers of Jesus)

Closed networks or open networks?

An update on the revolution: Be hopeful

DISCUSS

Take a few minutes with your group members to discuss what you just watched and explore these concepts in Scripture. Use the following questions to help guide your discussion.

1. What impacted you the most as you watched Randy's teaching on the Book of Acts?

2. When you think about a revolution (in light of Randy's teaching), what images come to your mind, and how can the church be a revolutionary movement of faith in our world?

3. **Read** Acts 1:4–8. What are ways that the Holy Spirit of God infused and empowered the church in the first century and how do you see that same Spirit alive and at work in the church today?

4. **Read** Acts 2:1–4, 14–18, and 40–41. This passage talks about the same Peter who had denied Jesus three times just a few days earlier. How did the Holy Spirit change Peter? How has the presence and power of God's Spirit brought change in your life?

5. **Read** Acts 2:42–47. Describe some of the behaviors, practices, and attitudes that marked the lives of the early Christians described in this passage. How are these things similar or different than what you see in the church today?

6. What are specific and practical things Christians can do today to increase **one** of these markers of church health?

   ○ Creating places for connecting together in larger community settings and smaller home gatherings

   ○ Building a community where people know they belong and are not alone

- Nurturing an environment of learning, praying, and growing in faith

- Encouraging acts of service and sacrifice for the sake of others

- Reaching out to spiritual seekers and loving them right where they are

7. Through all of his extensive studies, Dr. Stark learned that one of the most powerful ways that the church has continued to grow and change the world is through being an open network and not closed to new people. What are ways your church can avoid being closed and grow more committed to being open to people in your community from every walk of life?

MEMORIZE

Each session, you will be given a key verse (or verses) from the passage covered in the video teaching to memorize. This week, your memory verse is from Acts 1:8:

> *But you will receive power when the Holy Spirit comes on you; and you will be my witnesses in Jerusalem, and in all Judea and Samaria, and to the ends of the earth.*

Have everyone recite this verse out loud. Ask for any volunteers who would like to say the verse from memory.

RESPOND

What will you take away from this session? What is one practical next step you can take that will strengthen your church and unleash the staggering potential God has placed in the community of believers that you are part of?

PRAY

Close your group time by praying in any of the following directions:

- Thank God for the great things he is doing through his church around the world and right in the congregation where you are part of his family.
- Ask the Spirit of God to move in fresh and powerful ways in your church and in another church in your community.
- Pray for God to grow your passion for the church and your personal engagement in the life of your church.

SESSION ONE

Reflect on the material you have covered in this session by engaging in the following between-session learning resources. Each week, you will begin by reviewing the key verse(s) to memorize for the session. During the next five days, you will have an opportunity to read a portion of Acts 1:1–6:7 and reflect on what you learn, respond by taking action, journal some of your insights, and pray about what God has taught you. Finally, the last day, you will review the key verse(s) and reflect on what you have learned for the week.

DAY 1

Memorize: Begin this week's study by reciting Acts 1:8:

> *But you will receive power when the Holy Spirit comes on you; and you will be my witnesses in Jerusalem, and in all Judea and Samaria, and to the ends of the earth.*

Now try to say the verse from memory.

Reflect: We tend to rely on our strength, national might, personal wealth, relational alliances, and all sorts of other sources of power. Jesus was crystal clear that true power for God's people and his church come from the Holy Spirit. If we want to see the world transformed, it will only happen through our partnership with the Spirit of God. What are ways you can recognize the presence of the Holy Spirit in your life and unleash the Spirit's activity in your home and church?

DAY 2

Read: Acts 1.

Reflect: In the sixth verse of this passage the disciples gathered around Jesus and asked him if it was finally time for them to be in charge. Their nation was under the heel of the heavy boot of Rome. They believed that the Messiah would come as a political and military conqueror and crush the Romans and drive their forces out of the land. That was their expectation and dream. Even after three years of walking with Jesus, watching his ministry and listening to his preaching, they still did not get it. So, the risen Jesus patiently taught them again that his kingdom was not about political victory but spiritual transformation. They were not going to rule their land. Jesus was going to save the lost people of the world and they would be his partners in this mission. What are some of the misconceptions of what we want Jesus to do (often for us or against others) and how can you keep your heart and eyes focused on his mission and not your own desires?

Journal:
- What might the church look like if we let our focal point be on gaining political power and personal victory?
- What will the church look like if we stay locked on the mission of Jesus to seek and save the lost and be witnesses from where we are to the ends of the earth?

Pray: Confess where you tend to see Jesus as a tool to get what you want in terms of control, power, and authority over others. Ask for a humble heart that longs for Jesus to draw the lost sheep of this world to his shepherd-heart and prayerfully commit to join in his mission.

DAY 3

Read: Acts 2.

Reflect: Bold conviction is in short supply in our world and often in the church. In Acts 2:36–41 we see Peter, infused with the Holy Spirit, boldly calling people to repentance. He reminded them of their part in putting Jesus on the cross. He called them to turn from sin. He told them that the source of forgiveness is found in Jesus. Peter warned them. He pled with them. He called them to flee their wicked generation. Let's just say Peter laid it down! He held nothing back! Why are we often timid when it comes to sharing about Jesus? What would it look like if you were bold and confident in talking about your faith and the love, goodness, and truth of Jesus?

Journal:
- What sorts of risks was Peter facing when he spoke to this crowd in this manner and why do you think he was willing to count the cost?
- What holds you back from speaking the truth of Jesus? What consequences and costs might you face if you began speaking about your faith with increased confidence and consistency?

Pray: Ask the Spirit of God to grow your boldness when it comes to talking about Jesus and your love for him.

DAY 4

Read: Acts 3.

Reflect: For his whole life he had been a beggar. The man Peter and John encountered in Acts 3 had been placed near the temple day after day so he could receive alms from those going to worship. This was both his living and his life. Then, in one moment, everything changed! The beggar saw the disciples and made his request. "May I have some money?" Both Peter and John looked directly at him. They saw him not as a beggar but as a man who needed what only Jesus could offer. They asked him to lift his head and look at them. Then they made an offer he had never heard before. Peter and John did not give him what he wanted (money) but they gave him what he needed most (healing in the name of Jesus). How has God given you what you need most in the name of Jesus and how can you offer this same gift to others?

Journal:
- What are ways you settle for less than what God wants to give you?
- What are specific ways God has given you more than you ever dared to ask or dream through the gift of Jesus?

Pray: Praise Jesus for meeting you in your places of deepest need and thank him for the people in your life who have been conduits of God's grace into your life.

DAY 5

Read: Acts 4.

Reflect: In Acts 4:32–35 we get a snapshot of the heartbeat and culture of the early church. It is beautiful, inspiring, and shocking. These Jesus followers were unified in their hearts, minds, and behaviors. They shared with revolutionary generosity. They spoke freely of the goodness of their resurrected Savior. As they did this, the power of God poured through them in signs and wonders that pointed people to the goodness of God. Why do you think so many Christians stand in opposition to each other and what will help us live with increasing unity?

Journal:
- What are some ways you can help grow the unity in your church in terms of how people think (unity in mind)?
- What are some ways you can help grow the unity in your church in terms of how people feel and care for others (unity in heart)?

Pray: Ask God to humble the hearts of people in your church (including yourself) so that unity will grow and the world will be amazed by how you love each other and stand together in your faith.

DAY 6

Read: Acts 5:1–6:7.

Reflect: Imagine standing before the Supreme Court and knowing that they are not happy with you. They are powerful, they have authority to bring punishment, and you are their target. That's exactly what was happening to Peter and the other apostles in this chapter (v. 27 in particular). So how would they respond? Would they bend, compromise, and back off their mission? The answer to that question becomes absolutely clear in Acts 5:29–32. They doubled down! They ramped up! They followed Jesus and declared his truth no matter what the cost. How do you think you would have responded if you had been standing before the Jewish high court in the exact place where Peter and the apostles stood?

Journal:
- What are ways you can be tempted to compromise or back off when you feel pressured about your faith in Jesus?
- What are ways you can prepare to stand strong when the heat is on and people are pushing back against your faith?

Pray: Ask the Spirit of God to prepare you to be confident and articulate when you encounter people who disagree with or push back against your faith.

DAY 7

Memorize: Conclude this week's personal study by again reciting Acts 1:8:

> *But you will receive power when the Holy Spirit comes on you; and you will be my witnesses in Jerusalem, and in all Judea and Samaria, and to the ends of the earth.*

Reflect: Where should we be sharing our faith? Jesus calls us to be ready and willing to be a witness of his goodness, grace, and truth wherever we go. **Jerusalem** is our family, hometown, and the places we find ourselves day in and day out. **Judea** is our surrounding community. **Samaria** is one of the places most people avoid and where we might not want to go. The **ends of the earth** are exactly that . . . anywhere God might bring us. What is your Jerusalem, Judea, Samaria and ends of the earth? Take time right now to quietly commit, in your heart, to prepare yourself to be a witness of Jesus' amazing grace and life-changing truth wherever you go. Offer yourself to Jesus today, *"Savior and Leader of my life. Please open doors for me to be your witness today and every day of my life. For your glory and the sake of the world. Amen!"*

STICKS AND STONES

ACTS 6:8–9:31

God's mission to reach the world accelerated when his people were persecuted and scattered beyond the places where they were most comfortable. As God's church moved outward into the world, they loved people, treated them with dignity, and shared the message of Jesus.

WELCOME

All through history there have been plans, ideas, and actions that backfired. The desired result not only failed to come to fruition, but in many cases the opposite happened. For instance, in 1773 the British Parliament passed the Tea Act. It was a bill designed to give a monopoly on the sale of tea in the American colonies to British businesses. With the swipe of a pen and a new law the British believed they had won this particular financial battle. They thought they had put the colonists in their place. Until three tea ships had their cargo dumped into the Boston Harbor. Not only did the Tea Act not solve the immediate problem for the British, it became one of the catalytic moments that led to the American Revolution! Can you say, "Backfire"?

In 1902 the city of Hanoi, Vietnam had a serious problem with rats. Due to underground sewer pipes, the rodents ran wild below the city and spread everywhere. The leaders came up with a brilliant idea. They would give a small bounty for every rat that was killed. It became a cottage industry. But as time passed, the number of rats increased rather and decreasing. Why did their plan backfire? The political leaders did not want people bringing bags full of dead rats to city hall so they paid them for every rat tail they delivered. You might already have figured out what happened. Instead of killing the rats, the motivated and entrepreneurial rodent hunters were just cutting off their tails and letting the rats go free. This way they made money and the rat population grew . . . pretty clever. It was another historical backfire.

When the Imperial Japanese Navy Air Service attacked the US naval base at Pearl Harbor in Honolulu on Sunday, December 7, 1941, they sunk or damaged sixteen ships and destroyed 180 US aircrafts, took the lives of 2,403 Americans and injured 1,178. It looked like a massive victory for Japan who went on to declare war against the United States and the British Empire later that same day (the US was a neutral country at the time of the attack). History has gone on to show that this unprovoked and unannounced attack backfired as it brought American and British forces into the war. On September 2, 1945, The Empire of Japan signed an agreement of formal surrender on the deck of the USS Missouri in Tokyo Bay. That very ship is now a museum ship at Pearl Harbor and her bow faces the USS Arizona Memorial commemorating the attack on Pearl Harbor.

SHARE

Tell about a time you or someone you know experienced something that backfired or did not turn out how it was planned.

WATCH

Play the video for session two. As you watch, use the following outline to record any thoughts, questions, or key points that stand out to you.

Adele's sad story

Review of Session One

The value of women in the early church contrasted to the place of women in ancient Rome (Acts 6:1–7)

The care of widows -vs- abuse of widows

Protecting the unborn -vs- taking life in the womb

Loving children -vs- infanticide

Protecting young girls -vs- marrying off girls before puberty

Persecution of the church (Rome's massive backfire)!
(Acts 6:8–8:3)

Stephen's bold faith and preaching

Stephen's death and a vision of Jesus

Rome's plan backfires and the church spreads and grows

The church is a starfish and not a spider

The more things change, the more they stay the same (The first century and the twenty-first century)

What can God's revolution of faith look like today?

DISCUSS

Take a few minutes with your group members to discuss what you just watched and explore these concepts in Scripture. Use the following questions to help guide your discussion.

1. What impacted you the most as you watched Randy's teaching on Acts 6:8–9:31?

2. Adele's story opens our eyes to the sad reality that our society is becoming more isolated and many people fall off the community radar and are forgotten. What are ways that God's revolutionary people can care for each other (in particular other Christians who are hurting, marginalized, and often forgotten)? What are practical and specific ways that God's people can serve those in our community who don't have a church family but need compassion and care?

3. **Read** Acts 6:1–7. What were some of the dramatic contrasts between how the Roman Empire treated women and how the church loved and served women in the first century? What are ways you can honor and lift up women in your church and your community?

4. **Read** Acts 6:8–14 and 8:1. What kind of persecution did the Christians in the early church face as they tried to follow Jesus and share his love? What are ways that Christians are facing persecution and cultural conflict in our world today?

5. **Read** Acts 7:54–8:4. How did Christians in the early church respond to persecution, and what can we learn from their example?

6. What are some of the core beliefs and biblical truths of the Christian faith? (These are the things that make us distinctively Christian.) Why is it essential that we know and never compromise these truths?

7. When the church is a top-down clergy-led institution it is more like a spider that can be quickly snuffed out. When the church is centered on biblical belief and faithful ministry that is embraced by all the members, it is more like a starfish that can't be stopped! What are signs that a church is becoming more like a spider? What are indicators that a church is healthy and resilient like a starfish?

8. What are ways you can help your church become a healthy, resilient, and a revolutionary people of faith?

MEMORIZE

Each session, you will be given a key verse (or verses) from the passage covered in the video teaching to memorize. This week, your memory verse is from Acts 8:4:

> *Those who had been scattered preached the word wherever they went.*

Have everyone recite this verse out loud. Ask for any volunteers who would like to say the verse from memory.

RESPOND

What will you take away from this session? What is one practical next step you can take to share the love and message of Jesus in the places God places you in the flow of a normal week?

PRAY

Close your group time by praying in any of the following directions:

- Pray for your church to love and care for the forgotten and marginalized people who are inside and outside of the church.
- Thank God for the truth of the Bible and pray for hearts that love the Scriptures, minds that learn the truth of God's Word, and lives that surrender to the truth of the Bible.
- Praise God that he strategically and wisely places his people all over the world to share his love, truth, and Good News.

SESSION TWO

Reflect on the material you have covered in this session by engaging in the following between-session learning resources. Each week, you will begin by reviewing the key verse(s) to memorize for the session. During the next five days, you will have an opportunity to read a portion of Acts, reflect on what you learn, respond by taking action, journal some of your insights, and pray about what God has taught you. Finally, the last day, you will review the key verse(s) and reflect on what you have learned for the week.

DAY 8

Memorize: Begin this week's study by reciting Acts 8:4:

Those who had been scattered preached the word wherever they went.

Now try to say the verse from memory.

Reflect: Jesus was clear that his followers would bring the message of his truth and grace all over the world. But up to this point, most of them had stayed comfortably in their home base of Jerusalem. It was not until persecution came (which was meant to extinguish the church) that the Christians scattered. As they went out, the Jesus movement was ignited and spread like wildfire through Judea and Samaria. How has God used difficult times and struggles in life to grow your faith and move you to share his message with people you might have never even talked to?

DAY 9

Read: Acts chapter 6 and focus on verses 8, 10, 15.

Reflect: Stephen was an ordinary guy who loved Jesus and was filled with the presence and power of the Holy Spirit. We meet this godly man in Acts 6:5 and he is buried in Acts 8:2. We are honored to read one speech or sermon that he gave in front of the Jewish high court (the Sanhedrin) in Acts, chapter 7. He shows up on the pages of Scripture like a shooting star blazing across the sky and then he disappears. Yet his life made an impact. His sacrifice mattered (just read Paul's words in Acts 22:20). What were some of the traits in the life of Stephen that inspire you and what can you learn from his bold commitment to follow Jesus no matter what the cost?

Journal:
• How do you see God at work in and through Stephen in big and surprising ways?

- How do you see God moving in and through Stephen in humble and simple ways (remember what his calling and ministry was)?

Pray: Thank God for the people in your life who have served Jesus in simple and quiet ways and also for those who have been bold and sacrificial in their following of Jesus.

DAY 10

Read: Acts 7.

Reflect: Basic Sunday School 101. That's what Stephen brought to the highest court in the Jewish first century world. He was surrounded by some of the best minds of his day and these people knew the Scriptures front and back. What did Stephen do? He went back to the basics. It is like the famous Green Bay Packers coach, Vince Lombardi, on the first day of football practice. He would hold up the ball and say, "Gentlemen, this is a football!" Most of the players had played football as kids, in high school, as well as the college level. They knew what a football looked like. But Lombardi always started with the fundamentals. This is what Stephen was doing! He walked the scholars through the ABCs of faith. Why do you think Stephen focused on the basic history and story of the people of God?

Journal:
- What are the core and basic biblical beliefs that define the Christian faith?
- Why is it essential that we review and remember the core truths that the Scriptures teach?

Pray: Ask God for discipline to read his Word often and attentively. Pray for a mind that will remember, love, and share the simple truths of the Christian faith.

DAY 11

Read: Acts 8.

Reflect: There is a one-word term that has been used through the history of the church. It is, "simony." Simony is the act of buying or selling church position, offices, pardon or influence for money. It comes from Acts chapter 8. When Simon the sorcerer became a follower of Jesus, he was changed. He no longer wanted to use the demonic and dark spiritual power that he had wielded before receiving Jesus. But when he saw the power of the Holy Spirit alive in the disciples, he wanted that power for himself. Simon actually offered money to receive the power of the Holy Spirit. Peter rebuked him strongly and called him to repent. By the grace of Jesus, Simon humbled himself and asked Peter to pray for him. What are ways that simony can still happen in the church today? How do people try to buy influence and position in the church?

Journal:
- Why is the act of simony so repugnant to the heart of God?
- What are ways we can be sure this practice does not spring up in the life of the church?

Pray: Ask the Spirit of God to work in power in the life of your church and pray that the influence of money never sways the direction or leadership of your church.

DAY 12

Read: Acts 9:1–19.

Reflect: This is one of the most dramatic events in the New Testament. A Christian-hating man named Saul is right in the middle of his vendetta to destroy believers, churches, and the whole Jesus movement. His life is focused like a heat-seeking missile on shutting down the ministry Jesus came to initiate in human history. By the powerful work of God and an encounter with the risen and living Jesus Christ, Saul became Paul and his life made a 180-degree U-turn. The killer of Christians became a radically committed follower of Jesus, a missionary, and eventually the author (through the inspiration of the Spirit) of almost half of the books in the New Testament. What are ways that the presence of Jesus in your life has caused you to take a U-turn and live in a whole new way?

Journal:

- Who is a person you know that seems like they are heading away from God and fighting all that God would want to give them? How can you pray for and encourage this person to be open to a dramatic life change?
- What are areas in your life where you are moving away from God's plan and will for you? Would you dare to stop right now, confess, repent, and ask the Holy Spirit to empower you to turn and follow Jesus with new passion and devotion?

Pray: Thank God for how his Spirit has changed your life and led you in new directions.

DAY 13

Read: Acts 9:19–31.

Reflect: What a dramatic and shocking picture! Just a short time earlier, the great Rabbi Saul was in a position of power and authority. He had official letters from the High Priest in Jerusalem. He was empowered to arrest any Christian he encountered, man or woman, and bring them as a prisoner to Jerusalem to stand trial. Now his name was Paul. He was no longer the hunter, but he was the hunted! His articulate preaching and teaching were making an impact for Jesus, but his past colleagues were now wanting to arrest and kill him. He was hiding out in Damascus and his life was in danger. In Acts 9:25 we see a shocking picture. Paul is on the run and the only way to get him out of town is by lowering him in a basket through an opening in the city wall. Paul's journey to Jesus was a move from pride to humility. How has God allowed you to increase in humility and set aside pride as you have grown in your devotion to follow Jesus?

Journal:
- What are areas of your life where you still deal with pride and how do you think God feels about these attitudes and behaviors?

- What are ways you can humble your heart and live in ways that reflect the humility and gentleness of Jesus?

Pray: Pray for eyes to recognize where hubris is growing in your heart and life. Ask the Holy Spirit to give you strength and commitment to repent of this pride and grow in genuine humility.

DAY 14

Memorize: Conclude this week's personal study by again reciting Acts 8:4:

> Those who had been scattered preached the word wherever they went.

Reflect: When we read the word "preached" in this passage it would be easy to exclude ourselves from this activity. The word "preached" means that they declared, talked about, and boldly shared the story of Jesus. These were not preachers in a pulpit. They were ordinary Christians driven from their homes, living in new communities, and talking about Jesus wherever they went. What are ways you can talk about Jesus in the places you go in a normal day? Where is God scattering you as his loving and joyful messenger of his grace and love?

SAINTS AMONG US

ACTS 9:32–12:24

In the first century, the church spread outward from Jerusalem to the ends of the earth as the early believers recognized that people are often hurting, broken, fearful, and abandoned. Jesus' revolutionary people served, offered help, and modeled a life filled with hope, faith, and joy. As they did this, individuals, families, and entire regions opened their hearts to Jesus, the Savior.

WELCOME

Since Jesus established his church there have been saints among us. Ordinary Christians who have met the Savior, believe his Word, extend his love, and serve others like Jesus served them. This is as true today as it was two-thousand years ago when the church was first spreading across the known world.

Rosita is eleven years old and has loved Jesus for as long as she can remember. She has friends in her neighborhood and at school, but she is also in the habit of looking for kids her age that have been outcast and ostracized. She smiles at them, says "Hello," and stops to talk. Rosita invites those on the outside of social circles into her life, home, church, and heart. Because of her kindness and open arms, she has more than a dozen new friends who have come to follow Jesus through her example and stories of faith. Yes, there are still saints among us!

Daniel is an elder at his church, teaches junior high Bible study twice a month and is a manager at a local hardware store. He works hard and expects his employees to do the same, but he is also a great listener and shows real compassion to customers, employees, and others on the management team where he works. It is not unusual to see Dan praying for a customer or staying after work to help an employee learn a new skill that will help them be more effective at their job. He is truly a saint among us!

Hannah is a college student who studies hard, works at a local restaurant to help cover the cost of tuition and still makes time to serve at her church's food pantry twice a month. In the midst of a full life, Hannah says that one of the highlights of her month is joining other volunteers to organize and distribute bags of groceries to folks who are hurting and having a hard time making ends meet. At the food pantry, she is able to have conversations with people, pray for them, give words of encouragement, offer a free Bible, and provide good and healthy food. As she does this, she seems to always have a smile on her face and joy in her heart. Hannah is another saint among us!

SHARE

Tell about a Christian you know who loves people well, shows compassion to the hurting, and reveals the heart of Jesus in their daily interactions. How is this person a "saint among us" and how have you seen God use this person to reveal the love and the presence of Jesus?

WATCH

Play the video for session three. As you watch, use the following outline to record any thoughts, questions, or key points that stand out to you.

One boy's journey to Jesus

Life in Antioch (and many other ancient cities and towns)

Massive congestion of people

Utterly filthy

Disease and sickness

Crime everywhere

Natural and social disasters

The amazing impact of the church in a broken world (Acts 9)

God does not pick favorites and neither should we (Acts 10)

The church and grace of Jesus reaches the Gentiles
(non-Jewish people) (Acts 11:19–26)

Sharing with those in need and living generously
(Acts 11:29–30)

A third progress report (Acts 12:24)

Acts 29 . . . The story of the church is still being written

Lessons from a Gallup study

The positive and amazing benefits of Christian beliefs
and practices

What is your next step?

DISCUSS

Take a few minutes with your group members to discuss what
you just watched and explore these concepts in Scripture. Use
the following questions to help guide your discussion.

I. What impacted you the most as you watched Randy's teach-
    ing on Acts 9:32–12:24?

2. Tell about your journey to Jesus and describe one of the
    "saints among us" who showed you the heart of Jesus and
    told you about God's truth.

3. Randy gave some vivid and shocking background information about the city of Antioch and the difficult situation so many people were experiencing in the first century. How did the Good News of Jesus (brought through compassionate and loving Christians) impact people in the ancient world? What are some of the ways that God's love and message, when brought through caring and gracious believers, can bring hope and freedom to people in our world today who are dealing with their own "pain points"?

4. **Read** Acts 9:32–43. How did the early disciples reveal the heart of Jesus by showing compassion and love to the people they met? How did those people respond when they saw the grace and power of God revealed through ordinary people?

5. **Read** Acts 10:23–35. How was Peter learning that favoritism does not reflect the heart of Jesus? Why is it essential that Christians today learn this same lesson? What are ways that Christians can resist the temptation to show favoritism?

6. Randy says that we are living in Acts chapter 29. In the Bible, the Book of Acts has only 28 chapters. The church today is still writing the story of God's revolution of faith. Who is one person in your life you would love to see come to know Jesus Christ as their Lord and Savior? What is one Christlike action you can take in the coming days to reflect the love of Jesus for them?

7. Why do you think that people who hold to Christian beliefs, and who follow core Christian practices, are more accepting of people from different races, happier, quicker to help those in need, and more likely to extend forgiveness and live longer?

8. What are some of the biggest "pain points" in the lives of non-believers who live in your community? What are practical ways you, your small group, or your church can meet people in their places of pain and extend the love, care, and grace of Jesus?

MEMORIZE

Each session, you will be given a key verse (or verses) from the passage covered in the video teaching to memorize. This week, your memory verse(s) are from Acts 10:34–35:

> *Then Peter began to speak: "I now realize how true it is that God does not show favoritism but accepts from every nation the one who fears him and does what is right."*

Have everyone recite this verse out loud. Ask for any volunteers who would like to say the verse from memory.

RESPOND

What will you take away from this session? What is one practical next step you can take to serve, help, and love people in the middle of their pain so that they will see the heart and face of Jesus?

PRAY

Close your group time by praying in any of the following directions:

- Thank God for one of the people who pointed you to Jesus and reflected his love and compassion so that you could get a true picture of what it looks like to follow Jesus.
- Pray for Christian ministries and church programs you know of that are designed to identify pain points in your community and bring the amazing care of Jesus to people right at their place of need. Ask God to draw people to the heart of Jesus through these ministries.
- Confess where you or your church has let prejudice or favoritism get in the way of loving people who are different. Ask for a movement of repentance so that the Good News of Jesus can be released powerfully in your community to everyone with equal grace.

SESSION THREE

R eflect on the material you have covered in this session by engaging in the following between-session learning resources. Each week, you will begin by reviewing the key verse(s) to memorize for the session. During the next five days, you will have an opportunity to read a portion of Acts, reflect on what you learn, respond by taking action, journal some of your insights, and pray about what God has taught you. Finally, the last day, you will review the key verse(s) and reflect on what you have learned for the week.

DAY 15

Memorize: Begin this week's study by reciting Acts 10:34–35:

Then Peter began to speak: "I now realize how true it is that God does not show favoritism but accepts from every nation the one who fears him and does what is right."

Now try to say the verse from memory.

Reflect: God does not have favorites and neither should we. Jesus came and died for the sins of all who would believe and follow him. This is the lesson Peter learned when he encountered Cornelius and his family. They were not of Jewish descent but they hungered to encounter God and his only Son Jesus the Messiah. Because Peter was raised in a religious culture that believed that Yahweh was only the God of their people, he was shocked when it became crystal clear that God loves all people and Jesus' sacrifice on the cross was for people from every nation, tribe, and people. Is there favoritism hiding in your heart? If there is, confess it to Jesus who loved you long before you yielded your heart and bent your knees to him.

DAY 16

Read: Acts 9:32–43.

Reflect: Notice this simple progression. 1) Christians came to a new place or situation. 2) They identified a need, hurt, or place they could minister the grace and mercy of Jesus. 3) They went into action and did something that helped a person in need and pointed to the power and goodness of Jesus. 4) Many people in that area turned their hearts and their lives to the Lord Jesus (Acts 9:35 and 42). It is simple and beautiful! What might happen if all of God's people followed this simple progression whenever they entered into a new setting?

Journal:
- What are some new places or settings you might find yourself in the coming month?
- What are ways you could identify hurts, needs, or pain points in each of these locations or situations?

Pray: Ask God to help you see the needs around you everywhere you go. Invite the Holy Spirit to move you and empower you to help meet needs in his power and in the name of Jesus.

DAY 17

Read: Acts 10.

Reflect: When worlds collide, great things can happen! Cornelius feared God but did not know Jesus. He was a soldier in charge of other soldiers in the Roman army. Peter was Jewish and had worked for much of his life as a fisherman. He was a follower of Jesus and a leader in the early church. These two men could not have been more different! With that in mind, ask yourself, "Why would God give Cornelius a vison with specific instruction to reach out to Peter?" The Jewish law would not even allow Peter to enter the house of a Gentile. But God has a way of bringing together very different people to show the world that in Christ we can be family and stand united. Who are some of the very different kinds of people you have seen God bring together in your church?

Journal:
• How did Peter's attitudes and actions change after this encounter with Cornelius?
• What amazing things did God do because Peter was willing to break through some of the social and religious barriers that were keeping him away from people like Cornelius and his family members?

Pray: Ask God to bring people into your life and church so that you can continue learning that God does not show favorites. Thank God that people who are very different than each other can live in unity because of the grace of Jesus.

DAY 18

Read: Acts 11:1–18.

Reflect: "Who was I to think that I could stand in God's way?" That was Peter's question to the leaders and authorities in

Jerusalem (the corporate headquarters of the early church). When they heard that Peter had gone into the home of a non-Jewish person, they were outraged. That was against their man-made rules and regulations. But Peter did something very wise. He told his story . . . detail by detail. When they heard what had really happened and how God had moved in power, their hearts softened. As a matter of fact, they went from being critical (v.2) to praising God and giving their affirmation (v.18). Why do you think Peter's account of what happened had such a strong and immediate impact on the church leaders?

Journal:
- What are some of the man-made rules and regulations we have in the church today that can get in the way of us really reaching lost people in our community?
- How can we get over these hurdles and minimize the impact of things that stop the church from doing the ministry God has called us to do?

Pray: Ask God to make your church a place where human regulations never get in the way of God accomplishing his will in and through the church.

DAY 19

Read: Acts 11:19–30.

Reflect: What's in a name? Early in the church, some people referred to the growing number of disciples as "Followers of The Way." It was in the dirty, overcrowded, dangerous city of Antioch where the disciples were first called Christians. After a year of teaching, preaching, ministry, and countless acts of compassion (led by Barnabas and Paul) the name just stuck: "Christian." And, it has been used ever since. The idea behind the name is that these people were following Jesus the Christ. They were trying to be like him, love like him, and share his words with everyone. They were inviting all people to follow this Jesus Christ (The Messiah). When you call yourself a Christian, what does this name mean to you and others?

Journal:
- If a Christian is supposed to reflect the person of Jesus, what kinds of attitudes and actions should mark our lives?
- If people look at you as a reflection of Jesus the Christ, what will they learn about your Savior?

Pray: Ask God to help you look more like Jesus, love more like Jesus, care more like Jesus, and live more like your Savior.

DAY 20

Read: Acts 12:1–24.

Reflect: Do we really believe in miracles? We should! But often we can wonder if the miracles in the Bible really happened. This very serious story of persecution actually has some humorous moments. Peter is a prisoner in a Roman cell and was headed to what looked like certain death. While he slept, God was moving. God sent an angel to the cell (Miracle 1). A heavenly light flooded the cell (Miracle 2). Peter's chains fell off (Miracle 3). The angel talked to Peter (Miracle 4). None of the guards, men who knew that losing a prisoner was not an option, even saw Peter walk out (Miracle 5). The main gate to the prison just opened by itself (Miracle 6). Here is where it gets funny. Peter did not immediately believe what was happening. He thought it was part of the vision!

When Peter arrived where the disciples were gathered for prayer, the servant who came to the door heard Peter's voice on the other side. She was so excited that she ran to tell the disciples (but she did not open the door to let Peter in). When she told the disciples that Peter was just outside of the house, they did not believe her (v. 14). They thought she was out of her mind. They thought, maybe Peter had been killed already and it was his angel. While this was happening, Peter kept knocking! They would not believe it was Peter until they saw him.

Why do you think so many people had a hard time believing what was happening to Peter (including Peter himself)?

Journal:
- Do you believe the miracles in the Bible really happened? Why or why not?
- Why is it important that Christians believe in the miraculous and why is this a central part of our faith?

Pray: Ask God to help you read his Word with a deep confidence that the Maker of heaven and earth is able to do all things, including miracles.

DAY 21

Memorize: Conclude this week's personal study by again reciting Acts 10:34–35:

> *Then Peter began to speak: "I now realize how true it is that God does not show favoritism but accepts from every nation the one who fears him and does what is right."*

Reflect: We all know that Jesus came to save us from our sins. The problem is that many of us have a secret feeling that God is only interested in sinners who are like us. We can become tribal or even racist. Those who are very different than us can seem intimidating and we might not want them in our church or as part of the family of God. Jesus loves the outcast, the forgotten, and people who we might avoid. It is time for each one of us to ask the Holy Spirit to root out any attitude in our heart or practice in our life that pushes people away because they are different. God accepts people from every nation in the world and so should we. How can you become more loving, inviting, and compassionate toward people who are very different than you?

THE POWER OF GRACE

ACTS 12:25–16:5

God's revolution of faith flows through Christians who understand grace and share it freely. So much in the ancient world and our modern world is antithetical to the goodness and kindness of God. When Christians live in grace and extend it freely to others, people will see Jesus and hunger for what only he can give.

WELCOME

When you look back over your life, with piercing honesty, there are plenty of things to regret. We all have shady places in our past and specific things we would rather forget and keep hidden from others. We have spoken words that cut like a knife and damaged the souls of people who angered us . . . sometimes the people closest to us. Our minds have entertained thoughts and scenarios that would make us blush if others knew what ran through the hallways of our imagination. Our actions have dishonored God, hurt others, and embarrassed us. The list could go on and on.

The good news is that Jesus came to wash these sins away, bear our shame on the cross, and heal our broken lives. The apostle Paul understood grace so deeply because he never forgot what Jesus saved him from. Paul orchestrated the persecution and execution of Christians. He had ravaged churches. He had worked against the mission of Jesus and had grieved the Holy Spirit of God. Because of this Paul referred to himself as, the worst of sinners (1 Timothy 1:15). His profound awareness of his past sin made him intensely aware of the power of God's grace.

In the middle 1700s, there was a slave trader with the simple and common name John. He was both an investor in the slave trade and the captain of slave ships. He sold human beings who were made in the very image of God as if they were cattle. With time, John encountered God and came to faith in Jesus as the grace-filled Savior. He went on to enter ministry and spend the rest of his life preaching, teaching, and writing songs of worship and praise.

John lived with a deep awareness of his evil past and the power of grace to cover his sins. He wrote a worship hymn that is still known and sung by many today. There are people who do not profess faith in Jesus but they know and love this song. Here is the first verse:

> *Amazing grace how sweet the sound*
> *That saved a wretch like me*

I once was lost, but now I'm found
Was blind but now I see

When John Newton, the writer of Amazing Grace, was drawing near the end of his life he still held the truth of grace in his heart. His sight was failing, he was barely able to speak, and was losing his memory. As he sat with a friend, John spoke these poignant words, "I remember two things: that I am a great sinner, and that Christ is a great Savior."

SHARE

Tell about a time you had a deep sense of God's amazing grace toward you.

WATCH

Play the video for session four. As you watch, use the following outline to record any thoughts, questions, or key points that stand out to you.

Grace and a bee

Gentiles and the grace of God

Paul and Barnabas at the synagogue and doing ministry in
Antioch (Acts 13:13–52)

Bringing the message of grace to Lystra with a new model of
ministry (Acts 14:8–20)

Back to Antioch and Syria to report God's great work to the
church (Acts 14:21–28)

The battle for grace (Acts 15)

What's so amazing about grace?

Grace led to the spread of Christianity

Pagan worship of the Roman pantheon of gods-vs-the grace of God in Jesus

The Galatian Christians and their struggle with grace (Galatians 1:6–7 and 3:26–28)

Grace changes our view of class, the sexes, race, and everything else!

Grace can change the world

DISCUSS

Take a few minutes with your group members to discuss what you just watched and explore these concepts in Scripture. Use the following questions to help guide your discussion.

1. What impacted you the most as you watched Randy's teaching on Acts 12:25–16:5?

2. **Read** Acts 13:42–48. God was doing amazing things! People were responding to the movement of the Holy Spirit. Then, some people were filled with anger and jealousy. Why do you think these people were so upset about what was happening? How have you seen jealousy and envy bring pain and strife in relationships?

3. **Read** Acts 13:49–52. Paul and Barnabas had a habit of going first to the synagogues and preaching the truth about Jesus to their Jewish brothers and sister. They loved their people and wanted them to recognize Jesus as the Messiah and follow him. What happened to the focus and strategy of Paul and Barnabas' ministry as they faced another time of resistance? What were the different responses from the Gentiles and the Jewish leaders when they heard this?

4. **Read** Acts 14:8–20. The crowd of Gentiles (non-Jews) was passionately enthusiastic but completely wrong! They were looking through their own worldview and misunderstood what Paul and Barnabas were saying and doing. What was their misunderstanding and how did Paul and Barnabas try to correct it? In your own words, describe the message of grace and good news that Paul and Barnabas were trying to communicate to these spiritual seekers.

5. **Read** Acts 15:7–11. The fifteenth chapter of Acts is a decisive moment in the history of the early church. There were leaders in the church who believed (and were teaching) that before someone could be a good Christian, they had to become a good Jew. In this passage, the truth is declared. What specific truth about salvation comes out clearly in this passage?

6. **Read** Galatians 3:23–29. How does faith in Jesus unleash the grace of God and set aside human legalism?

7. What does it mean to say that in Christ there is "neither Jew nor Gentile, neither slave nor free, nor is there male and female, for you are all one in Christ"? What are ways we can change our attitudes and actions to show that we believe this is true?

MEMORIZE

Each session, you will be given a key verse (or verses) from the passage covered in the video teaching to memorize. This week, your memory verse is from Acts 13:47:

> *For this is what the Lord has commanded us: "'I have made you a light for the Gentiles, that you may bring salvation to the ends of the earth.'"*

Have everyone recite this verse out loud. Ask for any volunteers who would like to say the verse from memory.

RESPOND

What will you take away from this session? What is one practical next step you can take to receive God's grace more fully and share it more freely?

PRAY

Close your group time by praying in any of the following directions:

- Thank God for the many ways he has lavished his grace on you, including giving the gift of Jesus' sacrificial death on the cross for your sins.
- Ask the Holy Spirit to open your eyes to see places and situations where you can extend grace to people who do not deserve it.
- Confess the reality that there are times you fail to receive or extend grace in the way that Jesus desires.

SESSION FOUR

Reflect on the material you have covered in this session by engaging in the following between-session learning resources. Each week, you will begin by reviewing the key verse(s) to memorize for the session. During the next five days, you will have an opportunity to read a portion of Acts, reflect on what you learn, respond by taking action, journal some of your insights, and pray about what God has taught you. Finally, the last day, you will review the key verse(s) and reflect on what you have learned for the week.

DAY 22

Memorize: Begin this week's study by reciting Acts 13:47:

> *For this is what the Lord has commanded us: "I have made you a light for the Gentiles, that you may bring salvation to the ends of the earth.'"*

Now try to say the verse from memory.

Reflect: You are a light for all the nations. Our identity matters! The best way to know who we are, as followers of Jesus, is to ask God. His Word gives us clear details about this topic. In Acts 13:47, we learn that God has commanded that we be a light for all those who are outside the family of God. That is your identity! You are to shine the light of Jesus in your home, workplace, school, social settings, neighborhood, and everywhere you go. When non-believing people meet you and talk with you, what strikes them and stays with them? Is it the light of Jesus shining brightly through you?

DAY 23

Read: Acts 12:25–13:12.

Reflect: Listen and follow! That is what Barnabas and Saul (Paul) did. Their hearts were open, they were praying and fasting. But they were launched on a powerful journey of ministry when the Holy Spirit of God directed them. If they had gone on their own initiative and in their own power, they could have never stood up to the spiritual forces that would come against them. But when they were sent by the Spirit, they were ready to stand strong in the power of God. What an example for us! We can and should fast, pray, and seek the Lord. Then, when the Holy Spirit leads us, we can go out in power and confidence. Where do you need the leading of the Holy Spirit in your life today?

Journal:
- What are ways you can seek the Lord and invite the Holy Spirit to guide you forward toward God's will in your life?
- How can you spend time praying and fasting with a focus on one specific area of life you are needing God's leading?

Pray: Ask God to give you commitment and courage to really take time to ask for his leading and pray for power to follow as the Spirit guides you.

DAY 24

Read: Acts 13:13–13:52.

Reflect: We must connect the then to the now! When the apostle Paul spoke in the synagogue, he began with a brief history lesson. Paul reminded these people of faith about the story of the people of Israel. From the captivity in Egypt to God's divine deliverance, to the season of wandering in the wilderness, to their entry into the land of promise, to the judges, prophets, and kings. In a whirlwind CliffsNotes presentation, the apostle reminded them of what they already knew. The big question is, Why? Why review the past? The answer is, knowing our past can help us walk well in the present and into the future. All through the Bible we see examples of this pattern. Why do you think God gives us so many examples of his people remembering his past leading and faithfulness as they moved forward?

Journal:
- What are some of the ways God has been faithful in your life over the past year?
- How can remembering these moments of God's presence help you walk forward in faith and courage?

Pray: Pray for a great memory. Ask God to help you carry the past in your heart as you follow him into the future.

DAY 25

Read: Acts 14:1–20.

Reflect: Sometimes wisdom says, "Stay!" Sometimes the best course of action is to run! When Paul and Barnabas did ministry in Iconium we see examples of both of these. Things started well in this time of ministry and many people came to faith In Jesus. Sadly, some of the local people who did not respond to the gospel decided to poison the well and fan the flames of conflict. They tried to drive Paul and Barnabas away.

What happened next was wonderful, they stayed there for a long time, teaching and doing powerful works of God. Their decision was to hang in there and ramp up the ministry. Later, things got even worse and some people in that area plotted to have the followers of Jesus killed. The response this time was different. They packed up and headed to another region to preach and do ministry. Sometimes wisdom calls us to stay and sometimes wisdom moves us on. How do you know when it is time to stay or move on?

Journal:
- What were times God gave you wisdom to stay put, hang in there, and keep pressing on?
- What were times the leading of the Spirit called you to wisely move on, close a door, or run for the hills?

Pray: Ask God to help you seek his wisdom each time you hit a point of conflict or tension.

DAY 26

Read: Acts 14:21–15:21.

Reflect: Christians might have different mission fields, but we serve the same Lord Jesus. Today's reading contains one of the most pivotal moments in the history of the early church recorded in the Book of Acts. In this revolution of faith, one of the big questions was, "Is Jesus the Messiah and Savior for the Jewish people alone, or for the Nation of Israel *and* everyone else?" Through prayer, deep conversation, debate, and theological discernment, the conclusion was that Jesus is for everyone. Once this was agreed upon, the leaders of the early church knew that they were all following the same Lord, but not all of them were called to reach the same groups of people. We need to remember this lesson today. Who has God put you near and given you a heart to reach out to with the love and good news of Jesus?

Journal:
- Why do you think God leads some people to reach a certain group of people and others to share his love with an entirely different group?
- How can you take a step deeper into sharing the love, grace, and truth of Jesus with non-believers in your life and circle of influence?

Pray: Ask God to give you opportunities to shine his light and scatter the salt of his love in the coming week.

DAY 27

Read: Acts 15:22–16:5.

Reflect: Even great Christian leaders have times they disagree. In the middle of this portion of Acts, we get a snapshot of some tension and dissension. We have been reading about Paul and Barnabas doing amazing ministry as a team. Now (Acts 15:36–40) they have a disagreement about John (also called Mark) joining them on the next leg of their journey. They could not come to a consensus. As a matter of fact, they got a bit heated and the final decision was to form two ministry teams and move in different directions. When you think about it, God used this moment of tension to multiply the ministry and create two teams where there had been one. Think about a time when God used a difficult or even contentious situation to bring about something good for his glory.

Journal:
- We know that God does not cause evil and he is not the author of bad situations. What he does is to bring good and amazing things out of life's messes. Make a list of some of the ways you have seen God bring good out of a bad time in your life.
- What is one tough thing you are going through right now and how might God do something redemptive through it?

Pray: Pray for God to surprise you through bringing good from situations that don't seem like the source of anything positive.

DAY 28

Memorize: Conclude this week's personal study by again reciting Acts 13:47:

> *For this is what the Lord has commanded us: "'I have made you a light for the Gentiles, that you may bring salvation to the ends of the earth.'"*

Reflect: What you do matters! According to this passage, God has commanded you to bring his salvation from where you are to the ends of the earth. That's a huge calling and mission! When you come to know and follow Jesus your life is about sharing the Good News of his salvation wherever you go. Where will God send you this coming week? How can you bring the story of Jesus, the love of God, and the hope of the gospel with you?

ELEPHANT OR VIRUS?

ACTS 16:6–19:20

The church was never meant to focus just upward toward God and inward toward each other. We were made to go outward to the ends of the earth. As God's people follow Jesus, the good news spreads everywhere. This was true in the ancient world and it is still true today.

WELCOME

It began as a conversation starter. Eventually, it became a popular game. Maybe you have played it. It is called, "Would You Rather?" When you have the right questions you can open the door for laughter, learning about others, and all sorts of fun human interaction. Here are some examples of "Would You Rather" questions:

- *Would you rather* be chronically under-dressed or perpetually overdressed?
- *Would you rather* have the ability to see ten minutes into the future or 200 years into the future?
- *Would you rather* have to sing out loud to every song you hear or dance to every song you hear?
- *Would you rather* have a photographic memory or an IQ of 200?
- *Would you rather* have to work every day in extreme heat or intense cold?
- *Would you rather* have a personal maid or a personal chef?

You get the idea. Each question reveals something about you, your personal tastes, your view of the world, your likes and dislikes.

You could ask similar questions about how you see the church. These questions would be revealing and help you get a sense of a person's tastes, heartbeat, and view of the body of Jesus. Here are some examples:

- *Would you rather* go to a church that sings all praise songs or only hymns?
- *Would you rather* be part of a small church where you know most of the people quite well or attend a large church that can offer many different ministries but there are a lot of people you don't know personally?
- *Would you rather* attend a church where the primary focus is growing believers in faith or a church where the driving goal was to reach lost people with the gospel?

- *Would you rather* attend a church that was more like an elephant or one that was like a virus?

OK, that last one might not make sense, but it will in a few minutes.

SHARE

Answer one of the "Would You Rather" questions in the Welcome part of this study. Tell why you would rather do what you chose.

WATCH

Play the video for session five. As you watch, use the following outline to record any thoughts, questions, or key points that stand out to you.

An elephant or a virus?

The spread of the Jesus virus (Acts 17)

Where it all started

The example of the spread of Jesus's good news in Thessalonica

A new vision of the Messiah (Isaiah 53:3–12)

Jealousy and conflict

How the Jesus virus changes everything (Acts 19)

People changed by Jesus impact economic realities

People in love with the Savior change the religious climate

Acts 29 . . . How the Jesus virus is spreading today

Passionate followers of Jesus impact a community in amazing ways

A challenge to God's people . . . be God's virus wherever you go

DISCUSS

Take a few minutes with your group members to discuss what you just watched and explore these concepts in Scripture. Use the following questions to help guide your discussion.

1. What impacted you the most as you watched Randy's teaching on Acts 16:6–19:20?

2. The love and message of Jesus has been spreading like a virus for over 2,000 years. How would the community where you live change if you removed every church (every follower of Jesus) and the ministry they do, the love they bring, and the truth they share?

3. **Read** Acts 17:1–4. As Paul and his ministry partners traveled from place to place, they spread the viral message of Jesus. They didn't just do nice things and live good lives but they boldly spoke words of truth. What was the clear message about Jesus that Paul preached in Thessalonica and every city he visited? Why is this message so important for the viral spread of the Christian faith?

4. **Read** Isaiah 53 slowly and reflectively. What do you learn about Jesus, the Messiah, from this prophetic section of the Bible?

5. When a Christian believes and understands the truth about Jesus revealed in Isaiah's prophecy it moves them to action. How can the message of the Messiah found in this passage compel a believer to tell others about Jesus? If a spiritual seeker hears these words and believes them, how could it change their life?

6. **Read** Acts 17:5–9. When the transforming and contagious message of Jesus changes hearts and impacts a community, things can get a bit messy. Describe the conflict and consequences that came as the viral truth of the Messiah began to take hold in the lives of people in Thessalonica. Tell about a time that tension and conflict arose in your relational world because the reality and truth of Jesus did not make sense to some people.

7. **Read** Acts 19:17–20. When conflict arose in the city of Ephesus and eventually calmed, it led to a wave of radical repentance, deep confession, and actions of change in the lives of the Christians in that region. What are ways we can repent, confess our sins, and lay aside things from our past life that are holding us back from fully following Jesus?

8. Randy told a story about two members of his small group who invested in an adopted girl by helping her develop reading skills over the course of a whole year. Their loving service and help made a life-changing impact. What are some different ways your small group members could pour into the lives of people in your church and community and reveal the presence and love of Jesus through these actions?

MEMORIZE

Each session, you will be given a key verse (or verses) from the passage covered in the video teaching to memorize. This week, your memory verse is from Acts 17:6:

These men who have caused trouble all over the world have now come here . . .

Have everyone recite this verse out loud. Ask for any volunteers who would like to say the verse from memory.

RESPOND

What will you take away from this session? What is one practical next step you can take as you seek to be part of God's contagious plan to spread his good news to the places you will go this week?

PRAY

Close your group time by praying in any of the following directions:

- Think about people who were hosts of the message of Jesus and spread his viral good news into your life. Pray that their example and lifestyle will influence you in your daily interactions with people who are still far from Jesus.

- Thank and praise Jesus, the Messiah, for coming as the humble and suffering servant who died for your sins rather than coming as a political and military conqueror to reclaim land and governmental control.
- Invite the Holy Spirit of the Living God to make you a carrier of the viral message of hope, grace, and salvation that is found in Jesus alone.

Reflect on the material you have covered in this session by engaging in the following between-session learning resources. Each week, you will begin by reviewing the key verse(s) to memorize for the session. During the next five days, you will have an opportunity to read a portion of Acts, reflect on what you learn, respond by taking action, journal some of your insights and pray about what God has taught you. Finally, the last day, you will review the key verse(s) and reflect on what you have learned for the week.

DAY 29

Memorize: Begin this week's study by reciting Acts 17:6:

These men who have caused trouble all over the world have now come here . . .

Now try to say the verse from memory.

Reflect: How has Jesus turned your world upside down? He has a way of doing that. Jesus did not come to make a few minor adjustments in the lives of his people. He did not leave heaven just to bring us a hot cup of cocoa and make our lives comfortable. The Savior of the world came to offer us a total new existence. That is why Jesus said we must be born again (John 3:7). Take some time this week to reflect on some of the ways your relationship with Jesus is still turning your life upside-down.

DAY 30

Read: Acts 16:6–15.

Reflect: God closes doors and God opens doors. The question is, do we notice when our Lord is doing this? Paul and his companions were traveling all around their world bringing the good news of Jesus. Then, in what seems like a strange way, God closes a door and says that they should not go to Asia and do ministry at that time (Acts 16:6). Why would God close a door to ministry? The answer is right in front of us.

As God was closing one door, he was opening another. There was a powerful vision and call to do ministry in Macedonia (Acts 6:9). These faithful servants could not be in two places at once. So, the Spirit of God made their next step clear. Do you believe God still leads his people to the places he wants them to go and serve?

Journal:
- Think back through your life and make a list of times God has closed a door so he could keep you on the right track to follow and honor him.
- Write down a couple of times you really sensed God was nudging or leading you in a specific direction. How did God lead you closer to his heart and his will for your life?

Pray: Invite the Holy Spirit to close and open doors so that you can walk the path that most honors him.

DAY 31

Read: Acts 16:16–40.

Reflect: If God really loves us and we are walking in his perfect will, everything will go our way, the road will be smooth and lined with beautiful flowers, and all of our back pain will instantly disappear, right? Maybe not. In today's passage, we see Paul and his ministry team faithfully loving people and preaching the good news of Jesus. What results is not painless and perfect peace. Instead, their faithful obedience leads to conflict, abuse, imprisonment, and physical pain. What is going on here? Where is the tender God of love? Well, we see God's presence and care all over this passage. What were some of the signs of God's grace and presence in the life of Paul, his companions, the jailor, and his family?

Journal:
- When did God lead and guide you into a situation that was hard, challenging, and even left some scars?
- What good things did God accomplish through your sacrifice of following him even when it was difficult?

Pray: Ask God to lead you into situations where you can shine his light and share his love in his power . . . no matter what the cost.

DAY 32

Read: Acts 17.

Reflect: When you share your faith, start where people are, not where you would like them to be. All through the Bible we see God's people shining the light of Jesus and declaring the good news of the Savior. When Jesus did this, he always contextualized the message for the person or group that was listening. Peter did the same thing. So did Paul. When in Athens, do as the Athenians do! So, when Paul preached and shared his faith in the Areopagus (Acts 17:22) he did it in a way that connected for those people. He quoted their poets, noticed their religious practices, and spoke like a philosopher. This was not compromise or acquiescing to their religion. It was strategic and incarnational ministry. He met them where they were and sought to lead them closer to the true Savior of the world. What are some of the ways you can incarnate and contextualize so that you are more effective in sharing the life-changing message of Jesus?

Journal:
- What are some of the groups of people you will be around in the next month? How do they think, speak, and live? What are ways you can share Jesus with language they will understand?

- How has God uniquely made you to share the grace and truth of Jesus with people he has placed in your life?

Pray: Ask God for increasing opportunities to share your story of following Jesus and to do it in a way that really connects for them.

DAY 33

Read: Acts 18:1–17.

Reflect: Serving Jesus can be exhausting! Following the Savior is not always easy. Sometimes God gives us a season of protection, rest, and refreshment. That's what we see in today's passage (Acts 18:9–11). After a lot of conflict and tension in ministry, God gives Paul a vision and assures him that a time of safety, community, and peaceful ministry would be just ahead. What a comfort this must have been! What is wonderful is that it lasted for a year and a half. How have you seen God give you times of rest for your soul and refreshment for your body?

Journal:
- How are you doing right now? Are you feeling full, charged up, and refreshed? Are you feeling tired, depleted, and weary?
- If you are feeling empty and need a time of filling up, make a list of things that refresh your soul and then, do some of them.

Pray: Thank God for the refreshment he brings into your life and ask him to fill you up if you are feeling depleted.

DAY 34

Read: Acts 18:18–19:20.

Reflect: Mostly, but not totally! That would be a good way to describe the life and faith of Apollos (Acts 18:24–26). He was passionate about Jesus. He had studied the Scriptures hard. Apollos had been well trained. His speaking style was dynamic and effective. Most of his theological foundation was solid as a rock. Here's the problem. His belief system was only *mostly* accurate. That means it was *partially* inaccurate. What happens next is beautiful! A husband-and-wife ministry team pulls Apollos aside and gently corrects and trains him. They see his gifts and passion but they also recognize that Apollos needs some specific coaching and they offer it with humble hearts. Have there been times when someone loved you enough to correct and redirect you gently?

Journal:
- Who are people in your life who have lovingly corrected and trained you in the things of faith? Have you ever taken time to thank them? If not, do so soon.
- Who are people God has placed in your life that you can gently correct and encourage to walk more fully with Jesus?

Pray: Ask God to give you courage and the right spirit to correct others gently when they are mostly in line with God's Word but partially off track.

DAY 35

Memorize: Conclude this week's personal study by again reciting Acts 17:6:

> *These men who have caused trouble all over the world have now come here . . .*

Reflect: The early followers of Jesus were accused of living in ways and saying things that turned things upside-down. When Jesus entered the lives of ordinary people, hearts were flipped over, homes were transformed, cities were changed for the better, and the world was turned upside-down. When was the last time you were accused of bringing trouble and dramatic change wherever you go? What are some ways God can use you and the faith that is transforming your life to have an altering impact on the people and community around you?

CRY UNCLE

ACTS 19:21-28:31

The journey of following Jesus is paved with moments of humble surrender. From the first time we cry, "Jesus is Lord" until every knee in heaven and on earth and under the earth bows down to the Savior, our faith is about complete and absolute surrender to the will of God. This was true in the first century when the church was born and spread around the world. It is still true today.

WELCOME

In kid's sports, there is a point where a game has gone from a fun competition to a public athletic slaughter. A team of eight-and-nine-year-old football players are down by forty-nine points before halftime. A girl's five-and-six-year-old soccer team is losing by sixteen goals to zero in the first fifteen minutes of the game. You get the picture. In these moments the coach of the team that is getting hammered can throw in the proverbial towel. A mercy rule can be invoked. In a moment like this, surrender could be the best thing.

When an alcoholic has gone so deep into their addiction that relational bridges have been burned, they have lost another job, their health is compromised and their marriage is hanging on by a thread, it is time to surrender. When this person hits the bottom and has nowhere to look but up, there is hope. When a sincere moment of surrender comes, it could actually save their life!

Picture a couple of Christian men sitting with a close friend for a time of intense confrontation. They have watched over the past year as a Christian brother has been getting progressively entangled in an emotional affair with a woman at his work. He has not yet left his wife or ended up in a hotel room with the other woman, but they all know where this thing is headed. As these friends engage in this time of intervention and call their Christian brother to make a change, they are inviting him to surrender. "Admit you are on the wrong path. Turn your heart back to your wife. Don't take another step down this slippery slope." With sincere hearts and tears in their eyes, they challenge him. If he surrenders and repents, there is still hope. If he ignores them, disaster is on the horizon . . . closer than any of them realize!

Too often we think of surrender as a bad thing. To "Cry Uncle" seems like a sign of weakness. But, when we are surrendering to God's will, it is the best thing we can do. Surrender is a blessing and gift that every follower of Jesus needs to embrace freely.

SHARE

Tell about a time you surrendered what you wanted or were doing so that you could follow God's will and plan for your life. What made it hard to surrender and why were you glad when you finally did it?

WATCH

Play the video for session six. As you watch, use the following outline to record any thoughts, questions, or key points that stand out to you.

Cry Uncle

When Saul (Paul) finally surrendered to God (Acts 7–9)

A story of ultimate surrender (Acts 19–28)

Acts 19—Paul's commitment to the "ends of the earth" (Rome)

Acts 20—A surrender of relationships and life

Acts 21—Warnings about the cost of fully surrendering to Jesus

Acts 22—Surrendered but not senseless

Acts 23—God's divine presence in our times of surrender

Acts 24—When surrender leads to witness and impact for Jesus

Acts 25—Bold surrender and big influence

Acts 26—Human surrender and divine deliverance

Acts 27—The witness of a surrendered life

Acts 28—When you reach the goal, keep surrendering

Acts 29—We are still writing the story of the church

Say yes and surrender to Jesus and do it now!

DISCUSS

Take a few minutes with your group members to discuss what you just watched and explore these concepts in Scripture. Use the following questions to help guide your discussion.

1. What impacted you the most as you watched Randy's teaching on Acts 19:21–28:31?

2. Randy told a personal story about being forced to "Cry Uncle" and surrender to his big brother. What is the difference between being forced to "Cry Uncle" and making a conscious decision to surrender to what God wants for you?

3. **Read** Acts 20:22–38 (Read this slowly and let yourself be captured by the real human drama and feelings that are contained in this portion of Scripture). What do you learn about the things Paul knew he would face as he surrendered to Jesus and followed his leading? Why did Paul believe his sacrifice was worth enduring?

4. What warnings and exhortations did Paul give to these people that he loved so much (Acts 20:25–31)? How was Paul calling them to sacrifice and surrender?

5. **Read** Acts 26:19–29. How do you see the boldness and power of the Holy Spirit working through Paul in his encounter with these political leaders? What do you learn from Paul's example of surrendering to God's leading when he shares the gospel and interacts with King Agrippa?

6. **Read** 2 Timothy 4:6–8. Paul surrendered to Jesus over and over after his conversion. Now he is drawing near to the end of his life and he writes these honest words as he looks back and looks forward. What does Paul see as he looks back and what does he anticipate as he looks forward?

7. What are some of the ways you can be sure to fight the good fight, finish the race well, and keep the faith? How can your group members pray for you and cheer you on as you do this?

MEMORIZE

Each session, you will be given a key verse (or verses) from the passage covered in the video teaching to memorize. This week, your memory verse is from Acts 20:24:

> *However, I consider my life worth nothing to me; my only aim is to finish the race and complete the task the Lord Jesus has given me—the task of testifying to the good news of God's grace.*

Have everyone recite this verse out loud. Ask for any volunteers who would like to say the verse from memory.

RESPOND

What will you take away from this session? What is one practical next step you can take as you seek to surrender your life to the will and ways of Jesus?

PRAY

Close your group time by praying in any of the following directions:

- Thank God for the Christians who have gone before you and who have surrendered their hearts, dreams, and lives for the work of Jesus. If they have impacted you personally, thank God for sending them into your life.
- Ask the Holy Spirit of God to help you say "Uncle" and surrender your life to Jesus more and more with each passing day.
- Pray for opportunities to share your story of faith with bold confidence in the coming week.

SESSION SIX

R eflect on the material you have covered in this session by engaging in the following between-session learning resources. This week, you will begin by reviewing the key verse(s) to memorize for the session. During the next three days, you will have an opportunity to read a portion of Acts, reflect on what you learn, respond by taking action, journal some of your insights, and pray about what God has taught you. Finally, the last day, you will review the key verse(s) and reflect on what you have learned for the week.

DAY 36

Memorize: Begin this week's study by reciting Acts 20:24:

> *However, I consider my life worth nothing to me; my only aim is to finish the race and complete the task the Lord Jesus has given me—the task of testifying to the good news of God's grace.*

Now try to say the verse from memory.

Reflect: Paul is not saying that he did not value his own life. What he is saying is that compared to sharing the good news of Jesus, concern for his own life seemed very small. When you think about your life, what is the race you are running? What task has Jesus given you? When you finish this life, what is the legacy you believe God wants you to leave? Do all you can to invest your energy, resources, and heart in the things that will accomplish that mission.

DAY 37

Read: Acts 19:21–22:29.

Reflect: Tell your story and his story! When Paul finally arrives in Jerusalem, he just kept on doing what he had always been doing. New place, same message! Paul loved to tell his story about how Jesus had reached him, loved him, forgiven him, and led him (Acts 21:37–22:21). In the middle of Paul's story was always the story of Jesus. Do you know how to tell your story of how God reached you and the grace of Jesus transformed you? Are you ready to share your journey to faith in a way that is winsome, clear, and impactful?

Journal:
* Write out your personal story of how you came to faith in Jesus and be sure to include the simple account of the life, death, resurrection, and grace of Jesus within your story.

- Take time to write out a few accounts of how God is at work in your life right now . . . protecting, providing, leading, and revealing his love and grace.

Pray: Ask God to give you opportunities to share your stories with friends and family members who are still far from Jesus.

DAY 38

Read: Acts 22:30–25:22.

Reflect: Be willing to suffer and sacrifice for Jesus when it will bring him honor and advance the work of his kingdom. But, don't just suffer for no reason. In today's reading, you might have been struck by Paul's response to the Roman commander who was about to have Paul flogged and interrogated (Acts 22:22–29). Paul played the "I'm a Roman citizen card" and everyone backed off. Here is the big question, "Why didn't Paul do this same thing back in chapter 16 when he was being beaten in the city of Philippi?" He could have stopped it that time as well. It seems that Paul had a sense that his suffering would have a redemptive impact in Philippi so he let it happen

(Acts 16:22–24). If you read on in Philippians chapter 16 you see that God did amazing things through Paul's willingness to suffer for the gospel. How can you know when suffering might honor Jesus and when it is suffering that should be avoided?

Journal:
- When was a time that you (or someone you know) were willing to face shame, rejection, pain, or some other suffering for the sake of honoring Jesus?
- How did God use your suffering to bring glory to God or growth in your life?

Pray: Pray for wisdom to know when you should willingly suffer pain or injustice for the sake of Jesus.

DAY 39

Read: Acts 25:23–28:31.

Reflect: To the end of the earth and beyond! Paul finally made it to Rome, the center of the ancient world. From there, the good news of the gospel could spread everywhere. The end of the Book of Acts is a powerful and beautiful picture of

Paul teaching, meeting with groups of people, and continuing to do all he could to win people to the heart of Jesus, the Messiah (Acts 28:23–31). With thoughtful and gentle boldness, he invited everyone he met to embrace Jesus. When we come to the end of the Book of Acts, it is really a new beginning. Christians today live in Acts chapter 29. We are now the ones who bring the life-transforming truth of the Savior to the world. The revolution of faith will not end until Jesus comes again in power and glory. Until that day, our call is to tell the story of God's love revealed in Jesus the Christ as we are filled with the power of the Holy Spirit.

Journal:
- What are ways you are seeing the ministry of your church fulfilling the call of Jesus to bring a witness of his saving power right where they are and to the ends of the earth?
- How can you increase your engagement in the revolutionary faith movement of Jesus through the local church you are part of?

Pray: Pray for your life and the ministry of your church to be ignited in fresh ways with the revolutionary power and message of Jesus.

DAY 40

Memorize: Conclude your forty-day personal study by again reciting Acts 20:24:

> *However, I consider my life worth nothing to me; my only aim is to finish the race and complete the task the Lord Jesus has given me—the task of testifying to the good news of God's grace.*

Now try to say this verse completely from memory.

Reflect: You are living in Acts chapter 29. Believers in Jesus the Messiah are writing new stories of God's presence and power every day. His revolution of faith will keep changing lives, marriages, homes, workplaces, schools, neighborhoods, cities, and the world. Step into the adventure. Be God's revolutionary. Proclaim the kingdom of God and share about the Lord Jesus Christ every chance you get (Acts 28:31). There is no better way to live and there is no better way to die!

LEADER'S GUIDE

Thank you for your willingness to lead your group through this study! What you have chosen to do is valuable and will make a great difference in the lives of others. The rewards of being a leader are different from those of participating, and we hope that as you lead you will find your own walk with Jesus deepened by this experience.

This study on Acts in the *40 Days Through the Book* series is built around video content and small-group interaction. As the group leader, think of yourself as the host. Your job is to take care of your guests by managing the behind-the-scenes details so that when everyone arrives, they can enjoy their time together. As the leader, your role is not to answer all the questions or reteach the content—the video and study guide will do that work. Your role is to guide the experience and cultivate your group into a teaching community. This will make it a place for members to process, question, and reflect on the teaching.

Before your first meeting, make sure everyone has a copy of the study guide. This will keep everyone on the same page and help the process run more smoothly. If members are unable to purchase the guide, arrange it so they can share with other members. Giving everyone access to the material will position this study to be as rewarding as possible. Everyone should feel free to write in his or her study guide and bring it to group every week.

SETTING UP THE GROUP

Your group will need to determine how long you want to meet each week so you can plan your time accordingly. Generally, most groups like to meet for either sixty minutes or ninety minutes, so you could use one of the following schedules:

SECTION	60 MINUTES	90 MINUTES
WELCOME (members arrive and get settled)	5 minutes	5 minutes
SHARE (discuss one of the opening questions for the session)	5 minutes	10 minutes
READ (discuss the questions based on the Scripture reading for the session)	5 minutes	10 minutes
WATCH (watch the video teaching material together and take notes)	15 minutes	15 minutes
DISCUSS (discuss the Bible study questions based on the video teaching)	25 minutes	40 minutes
RESPOND/PRAY (reflect on the key insights, pray together, and dismiss)	5 minutes	10 minutes

As the group leader, you will want to create an environment that encourages sharing and learning. A church sanctuary or formal classroom may not be as ideal as a living room, because those locations can feel formal and less intimate. No matter what setting you choose, provide enough comfortable seating for everyone, and, if possible, arrange the seats in a semicircle so everyone can see the video easily. This will make the transition between the video and group conversation more efficient and natural.

Also, try to get to the meeting site early so you can greet participants as they arrive. Simple refreshments create a welcoming atmosphere and can be a wonderful addition to a group study. Try to take food and pet allergies into account to make your guests as comfortable as possible. You may also want to consider offering childcare to couples with children who want to attend. Finally, be sure your media technology is working properly. Managing these details up front will make the rest of your group experience flow smoothly and provide a welcoming space in which to engage the content of this study on the book of Acts.

STARTING THE GROUP TIME

Once everyone has arrived, it is time to begin the study. Here are some simple tips to make your group time healthy, enjoyable, and effective.

Begin the meeting with a short prayer and remind the group members to put their phones on silent. This is a way to make sure you can all be present with one another and with God. Next, give each person a few minutes to respond to the questions in the "Share" section. This won't require as much time in session one, but beginning in session two, people may need more time to share their insights from their personal studies. Usually, you won't answer the discussion questions yourself, but you should go first with the "Share" questions, answering briefly and with a reasonable amount of transparency.

At the end of session one, invite the group members to complete the "Your 40-Day Journey" for that week. Explain that they can share any insights the following week before the video teaching. Let them know it's not a problem if they can't get to these activities some weeks. It will still be beneficial for them to hear from the other participants in the group.

LEADING THE DISCUSSION TIME

Now that the group is engaged, watch the video and respond with some directed small-group discussion. Encourage the group members to participate in the discussion, but make sure they know this is not mandatory for the group, so as to not make them feel pressured to come up with an answer. As the discussion progresses, follow up with comments such as, "Tell me more about that," or, "Why did you answer that way?" This will allow the group participants to deepen their reflections and invite a meaningful conversation in a nonthreatening way.

Note that you have been given multiple questions to use in each session, and you do not have to use them all or even follow them in order. Feel free to pick and choose questions based on the needs of your group or how the conversation is flowing. Also, don't be afraid of silence. Offering a question and allowing up to thirty seconds of silence is okay. This space allows people to think about how they want to respond and gives them time to do so.

As group leader, you are the boundary keeper for your group. Do not let anyone (yourself included) dominate the group time. Keep an eye out for group members who might be tempted to "attack" folks they disagree with or try to "fix" those having struggles. These kinds of behaviors can derail a group's momentum, so they need to be steered in a different direction. Model active listening and encourage everyone in your group to do the same. This will make your group time a safe space and create a positive community.

The group discussion leads to a closing time of individual reflection and prayer. Encourage the participants to review what they have learned and write down their thoughts to the "Respond" section. Close by taking a few minutes to pray as directed as a group.

Thank you again for taking the time to lead your group. You are making a difference in the lives of others and having an impact on the kingdom of God!

God the Savior

Our Freedom in Christ and Our Role in the Restoration of All Things

Study Guide
9780310134930

DVD
9780310134954

This study reveals how God's upper-story plan ultimately came to fulfillment through the birth, ministry, death, and resurrection of Christ. In the New Testament, you will read these stories—featuring characters such as Mary and Joseph, the Twelve Disciples, John the Baptist, Mary Magdalene, the Apostle Paul, and the central figure Jesus Christ—discovering how God has been weaving our lower story into the greater upper story that he has been writing.

THE STORY

POWERED BY ■ZONDERVAN®

READ THE STORY. EXPERIENCE THE BIBLE.

Here I am, 50 years old. I have been to college, seminary, engaged in ministry my whole life, my dad is in ministry, my grandfather was in ministry, and **The Story has been one of the most unique experiences of my life.** The Bible has been made fresh for me. It has made God's redemptive plan come alive for me once again.
—Seth Buckley, Youth Pastor, Spartanburg Baptist Church, Spartanburg, SC

As my family and I went through *The Story* together, the more I began to believe and the more real [the Bible] became to me, and **it rubbed off on my children and helped them with their walk with the Lord.** *The Story* inspired conversations we might not normally have had.
—Kelly Leonard, Parent, Shepherd of the Hills Christian Church, Porter Ranch, CA

We have people reading *The Story*—**some devour it and can't wait for the next week.** Some have never really read the Bible much, so it's exciting to see a lot of adults reading the Word of God for the first time. I've heard wonderful things from people who are long-time readers of Scripture. They're excited about how it's all being tied together for them. It just seems to make more sense.

—Lynnette Schulz, Director of Worship Peace Lutheran Church, Eau Claire, WI

FOR ADULTS

9780310458197

FOR TEENS

9780310458463

FOR KIDS

9780310719250

TheStory.com

The Life-Changing
Bible Engagement Experience
That Will
Transform
Your Church

Impactful, proven, trusted, and easy to implement, THE STORY is the gold-standard Bible engagement program for whole churches.

THE STORY

With curriculum and books for all ages, along with preaching resources, small group study, youth group activities, and parent helps, *The Story Church Resource Kit* is your complete resource for the entire ministry year.

FOR CHILDREN   **FOR CHURCHES**

9780310719755   9780310719274   Campaign Kit   9780310941538

With over 3 million sold, *The Story* tells the grandest, most compelling story of all time!

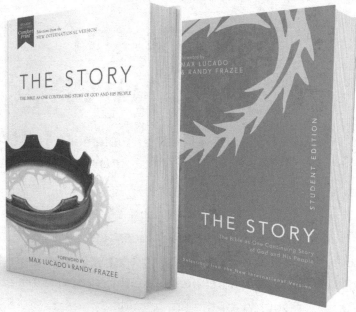

9780310458197   Student Edition: 9780310458463

God goes to great lengths to rescue lost and hurting people. That is what *The Story* is all about: the story of the Bible, God's great love affair with humanity. Condensed into 31 accessible chapters, *The Story* sweeps you into the unfolding progression of Bible characters and events from Genesis to Revelation, allowing the stories, poems, and teachings of the Bible to read like a novel.

Also available in a student edition with additional fun flipbook animation highlighting characters and story elements in the margins, and side tabs helping to bookmark your spot in the stories, poems, and teachings.

If You Want to Grow in Your Faith, You Must Engage God's Word

What you believe in your heart will define who you become. God wants you to become like Jesus—it is the most truthful and powerful way to live—and the journey to becoming like Jesus begins by thinking like Jesus.

Jesus compared the Christian life to a vine. He is the vine; you are the branches. If you remain in the vine of Christ, over time you will produce amazing and scrumptious fruit for all to see and taste. You begin to act like Jesus, and become more like Jesus.

In the **Believe Bible Study Series**, bestselling author and pastor Randy Frazee helps you ask three big questions:

- What do I believe and why does it matter?
- How can I put my faith into action?
- Am I becoming the person God wants me to be?

Each of the three eight-session studies in this series include video teaching from Randy Frazee and a study guide with video study notes, group discussion questions, Scripture reading, and activities for personal growth and reflection.

As you journey through this study series, whether in a group or on your own, one simple truth will become undeniably clear: what you believe drives everything.

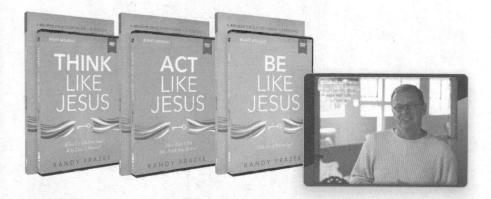

Available now at your favorite bookstore, or streaming video on StudyGateway.com.

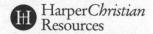